THE SNAIL'S SONG

ALTA IFLAND

Spuyten Duyvil
New York City

Acknowledgments

Grateful acknowledgment is made to the following publications in which these pieces first appeared: "An Eggcentric Man" and "Truth" in *The Redwood Coast Review*; "Turtle Tears," "Red Hoods and Sugar Dolls" and "The Story of the *a*-less Porcupine" in *Sentence*; "Song of the Rooster" in *Bateau*; "Trilingual Poem with Dead Swans" and "Bilingual Poem *avec Clichés*" in *Words without Borders*; "The Little Girl," "The Man in Quotation Marks," "Speaking a Foreign Language" and "The Reasonless Rose" in *Mission at Tenth*.

With drawings by the author

ISBN 978-1-933132-94-5

Library of Congress Cataloging-in-Publication Data

Ifland, Alta.
The snail's song / by Alta Ifland.
p. cm.
ISBN 978-1-933132-94-5
1. Prose poems, American. I. Title.
PS3609.F58S63 2011
811'.6--dc22
2011023771

THE SNAIL'S SONG

CONTENTS

I

II

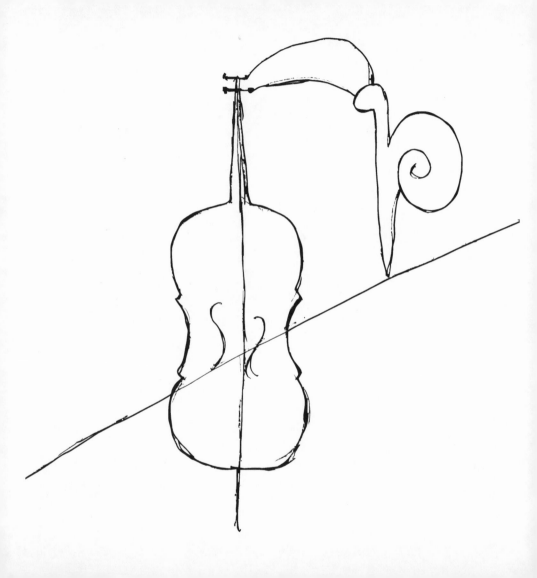

THE SNAIL'S SONG

I know a Snail like no other. In summertime he lives on a leaf whose tree is perched on a cliff above the blue-green sea; in winters he lives within himself. But be it summer or winter he sings and plays all day, he plays an instrument with no strings, no brass, no wind; he plays his own house. He is himself his own house, which he carries with him always, and he is himself his own instrument, which he plays with such passion that his friend, the Turtle, opens her eyes wide with astonishment, nodding and wiggling her green head. She too is her own house, though her house is no instrument. Not having the gift of song, the Turtle stays quiet by her friend, as he delivers his homemade melodies, which can't go anywhere because the house-instrument keeps them within its coiled shell. But how much song can a home take?

One day, filled with too much music, the shell cracked at the heart of its coil, and from that minuscule wound sounds spilled into the world. Day after day the Snail's song pours from the wound, and day after day his body, home and music are made anew, all one, in the secret darkness of the coiled, broken shell. His song comes from a broken home.

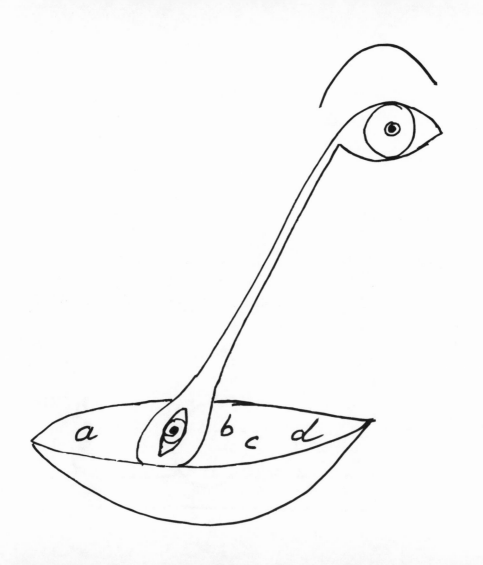

FIRST MEMORY?

She is three years old. Her parents appear not to be home; her nanny, an old woman with a funny name, isn't with her either, but she is surely in one of the other rooms.

The girl is sitting at a table too big for her, a bowl of soup before her. In her right hand she is holding a spoon also too big, with which she clumsily attempts to eat the soup. She drops the spoon on the table. The soup is too hot. She climbs on a chair and manages to seize from the wooden cabinet a cup or a jar—here the film fades and the image gets blurry—then off the chair and back to the table. How did she manage to fill the cup with water?

She pours the water into the bowl of soup and tastes again. Now it's too cold. And the taste is different. She looks at the soup as if it were an untamed animal with which no communication is possible.

MEDITATION AT NANZEN TEMPLE

I live in a rectangular, waterproof, gray suitcase. When it rains the leaves glow with droplets hanging at their edges, polished by the sun's reflection, heavy with a warm, inner smile. From my dwelling I don't see the leaves, but I do hear the rain. Its sound mimics a regular, muffled drumbeat anticipating a forthcoming ceremony. The drumbeat, in turn, mimics my heartbeat inside the tunnel that is my body. When it rains my body drifts inside a tunnel made of twigs, green leaves and gray rain. I part with my suitcase and take refuge in a drop of rain hanging from the tiled roof of Nanzen Temple. From there I can watch how sorrow slowly leaving my body drips onto the damp earth, drips like a split vein. Sorrow. Where does it reside? Where does it come from?

PAIN

It is crystal clear. It hollows us out, dressing our bones in pale-green acid, and it stuffs our mouths with aborted screams. It always comes from someone: a gift those we love most bestow upon us at intervals. Its biggest pleasure is killing hope. It smashes it and tramples on it until not a single crumb of hope is left. Then it enters us, slowly and deeply, as no lover ever did. It is the only thing that is entirely ours. Everything else—contentment, joy, love—is temporarily lent to us with a tremendous interest rate. But pain is ours, and we hold it in our bereft arms like the lover who is forever gone.

9

THE TOWER

The Tower stands above the dirty waters and the mice are playing in the waters deep in the waters and the cat is nowhere so the mice are playing and the princess is walking through the long dark halls seeping with grayness musty grayness and the princess is walking with her long gown rustling on the slabs of stone and on the stone like a heart of stone unseen by no one but the dark gray damp walls the princess is walking inside her loneliness of stone loneliness of stone stoneliness at home in her dark gray Tower with no one to see no one to hear no one but the mice in the muddy waters playing and playing hide-and-seek in the waters in the cave in the waters in the cave and the princess is walking inside her own grave lonely as a stone grave grave grave and somber as a stone in the grave and no one can hear no one can see and the princess is sighing and the sighs are flowing through the windows and down the gray damp walls down into the waters and the waters are rising up up up and the mice are crying and crying but the princess is silent mute as a stone and she goes down down down mute as a stone and no one can see no one can hear she goes down down and no one no one

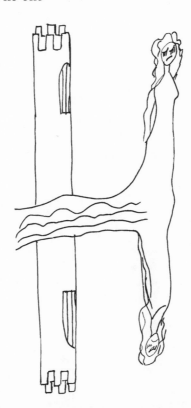

NOTHING INSIDE THE COFFIN

When they laid the tombstone above her she recoiled in a nook of the coffin "heavy with mummy-sadness" and clusters of uncried tears poured through her pores forming a stream and the coffin began to drift inside her veins but she knew it was an illusion because *she* was inside the coffin and she grew smaller and smaller until she was small as an apple and the stream under the coffin swelled and swelled carrying the coffin inside her eyes but she knew it was an illusion because *she* was inside the coffin and she grew small as a pea and the stream under the coffin was now a river on which the coffin drifted and the river began to overflow into the coffin and she thought she might drown but quickly quickly realized it was an illusion because in reality *she* was inside the coffin and she grew small as nothing and she knew it was real because that's what she was: nothing. Nothing.

13

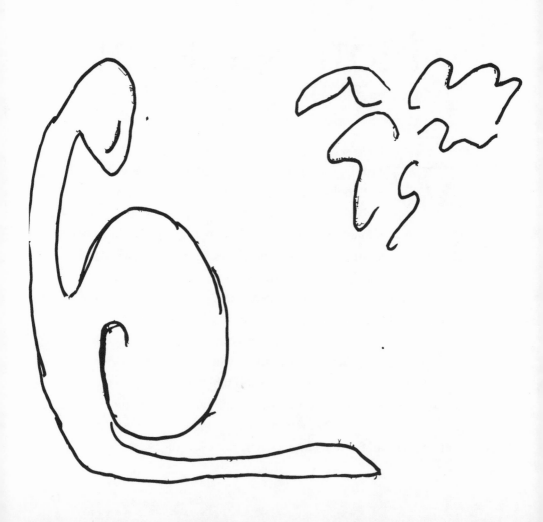

THE PATIENT BIRD

" I have a bird," he said.

"What kind of bird? What can it do?" she asked.

"Oh, nothing. It just stays there. It stays there for hours without doing anything. Still as a stone."

They watched the stone-like bird as it stood with its orange beak glowing in the dark and its ink feathers becoming one with the night. The bird was motionless. They called their friends so they could watch too, and they all watched and marveled at such a patient bird. Not a feather stirred on its still body. When they tried to touch it, its body slipped like a fish's, though it was the opposite of water. A stone-like body wrapped in soft feathers. What a patient bird, they thought. But when they least expected it, the bird suddenly moved and flew with its beak straight into their sockets, blinding them forever.

THE CHERRY SNOW

When she arrived at the end of the path with tall pine and eucalyptus trees on each side, she saw the two trees in front of the building with their branches extending alongside the entire façade, full with little white cherry flowers veined with light pink, and all the ground equally covered with white flowers. The whiteness radiated with snow-like intensity on the dark-green background of the forest. Heavy snow from the childhood amusement park in late December, heavy Transylvanian snow hanging from the seven dwarves' houses and from the trees decorated with unlit lights and long luminous icicles.

Beyond the forest the cherry flowers snowed silently with the bright silence housed at the core of snow, and the gray sad building stood with its halo of barely pink light, removed from space, hanging within a timedrop. And when she opened the doors and walked to the shelves lined with books, the building became once again the old library, and she could hear the silence of the outside snow enclosing it within its soft walls, and spilling onto the pages of the book she opened, and the book grew so very soft, radiating with snow-light, and the library began to smell like cherry flowers, and she could no longer tell the outside from the inside, and what or where she was.

THE STONE COLLECTOR

A man collected stones that he piled up into a tower in his backyard. The villagers said he wanted to bring the Tower of Babel into his yard, and mocked him. But what the man wanted was simply to enclose each sorrow within a compact, smooth, impenetrable stone, and thus to stop the flow of sorrow between things and beings. So he built a Tower of Sorrows, thinking that if he could gather all the sorrows in the world, he could make a stone bonfire and sorrow would vanish forever. Each night he stood by the Tower, putting stone atop stone, but he knew from the pain that never left him that tomorrow he would have to start all over again.

THE ROPE

I once knew a man who tried to make a rope of sand that would never break. Later he tried to hang himself, but the rope broke, oh it broke, and the man fell into a pit of tears. Then he tried to make a rope of water so he could climb back up, and a rope of water he made. He braided the tears like hair and made them into a long, thick rope, but when he was almost at the top, the tears dried up, and the rope dissolved into the air, and he fell back into the pit. Now the man was so desperate that he began to make a rope out of air, and he worked at it hours and days and weeks and months, and when he finished, he let himself slide up the thick, invisible rope of air, and he thus managed to ascend to the top. By now, our man was so weak and frail he could barely stand, so he was just about to sit down when someone gave him a push and yelled: "Old man! This is no place to sit and contemplate. Here we all make ropes. Take this sand and make it into a rope!"

So, the old man took the sand and made it into a rope with which he hanged himself, but the rope broke, etc.

THE LITTLE GIRL

The little girl had misty lips. She never spoke. When she opened her mouth the mist enveloped her little body and she dissolved entirely into herself. She was never there. The doctors were puzzled. They said that, biologically, there was nothing wrong with her and she should be able to speak, but when they tried to force her, only a long shriek came out. Things, too, disappeared when she touched them. She had two dolls made of rags, crushed patience and bitter sugar, but they too disappeared. Everything she touched vanished, except herself. Yet the only thing she ever wanted was to no longer be. She opened her mouth and let her body be swallowed by the mist, but something always remained: a leg, an arm, a nail. Something was always there, piercing through the mist, untouchable yet present: the pain of being.

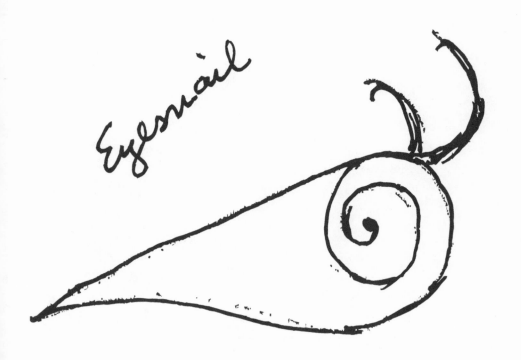

EYES

They enclose inside them everything that is outside them. Everything outside is for them subject for reflection. They are the mirror into which every single thing falls. Does this mean that, in reality, each thing is the exact opposite of what we see in our mirror? Since they are infinite deposits of images, the eyes are by their very nature the place where dwells the non-real. Whatever they see is sacrificed in a vertigo of nothingness that people used to call "soul" in the old days. Whatever they take in is transplanted to a kingdom of the beyond where being is transformed into non-being. The day when the eyes will have ceased to take in things, the soul will shrivel and die. For, in the end, having a soul is just a matter of how you look at things.

WATER AND STONE

"Water: what a word." It reminds me of stone and of time's play in its cracks. But water flows timeless, unhindered by the dust of hours. Unlike time, it is childless. Only in winter its "breath-crystal" freezes it in the present. Then, the slow work of time has begun in its liquid-heart. At times, when stillness fills the air, you can feel the becoming-stone of the orphan-waters. Orphaned and childless, the waters flow rootless.

THE WEB OF STONE

The bird brought twigs from a nearby tree, lined them with feathers like a winter coat, and little by little, by the end of the day it had made a nest. Then it spread its wings and sat in it, as if in an armchair. The bird was enjoying its nest so much it didn't notice when, as it opened its beak, a spider came out of it. The spider moved rapidly, weaving its thread amidst the trees' branches, and by morning it built an arabesque of white lace. The spider considered its work with pride, but when it tried to move away to see it from a distance, it realized it couldn't move its legs. They had turned into stone and the stone twisted in a myriad of convoluted stone threads—a web made entirely of stone. The spider tried to shake its legs, but its legs were still because they were of stone. Desperate, the spider looked around and saw that the web kept weaving itself, circling the trees and the houses, all the way up to the sky, and now everything was in stone: the trees, the houses, the sky, it was all a web of white-gray, unbreakable stone. And the spider began to sing: web of stone, web of stone, web of stone… And as he sang, the stone melted and he drowned in the liquid web of stone.

THE DONKEY AND THE PEARLS

Once, a donkey saw a pearl necklace hanging from a blossoming tree. Intrigued by its gleam, the donkey moved closer, extending a tongue rough as a cat's. With the tip of his tongue he touched the necklace, and facing it, saw his reflection in the shimmering mirror of its pearls. "Oh my, I am so handsome!" the donkey thought out loud. Upon which, the pearls, revolted, spat out his image in disgust. Ever since, the pearl has been known as the mirror in which no donkey can see himself.

THE MAN IN QUOTATION MARKS

He was a man in quotation marks. That is, his body occupied a space flanked on each side by a big, fat, curly quotation mark. Upward curls on the left, downward curls on the right. When he breathed, the curls fluttered under his breath, puzzled that the unreal, of which they were the guardians, pulsed with so much aliveness. When he spoke, his words could not be attached to any real place, but seemed to emerge out of themselves, like a unicellular organism reproducing through inner cellular division. They were all in quotation marks. His dreams were in quotes too. They were the dreams dreamt by millions of others before him, and very likely after him. Everything about him was repetition, and everything repeated is, according to grammar books, subject to be put in quotation marks. Yet, there was something about the way he breathed that was unrepeatable, unique. Something that puzzled the quotes again and again, infusing them with a wish to fly away and leave him naked in his unique aloneness.

THE CREATIVE CHIROPRACTOR

"Oh my God, your bones are all upside down!" said the chatty chiropractor. "We need to fix that!"

Then, she opened her tool box, and chirping happily about the energy in our bodies and the necessity of a proper alignment, took out a metallic instrument with a round end, and proceeded to tap on my knees. She then unscrewed all my bones, repositioned them and screwed them back.

"There," she said. "Now you are as good as new."

But ever since she did that, it is the world that appears upside down, and if I want to see it properly, I need to stand on my head with my legs up in the air. When I complained about this new annoyance, she answered, radiant with confidence:

"Oh, but think of all the progress you are making in yoga!"

Speaking a Foreign Language

I once knew a woman who could only speak a foreign language. That is, language was for her a body that, if too close, took the shape of a primitive, possessive, one-eyed, moon-struck beast. That's why, when she spoke, she had to move as far away as she could from the beast, from its claws on which the ancestors' blood dripped, sticky, dark, radiating motherly poison. That's why, when she spoke, she grew so light that her words could only come from an almost nonexistent body, an immaterial, orphan body, whose only ancestors were the ocean and the air. The ocean, whose salt flows in the blood, and the air, which is nothing, like—some day—our body.

THE REASONLESS ROSE

"The rose is without why, it blooms because it
blooms, […] it has no wish to be seen."
—Angelus Silesius

The reasonless rose knows that all that soars has no reason to rise yet in season or not roses relentlessly thrive less than reasonably. They seep and weep resting solely on trees with roots reaching deep as rampant seas rise to the shores ransacking bones from their ageless sleep. Their smell is redolent of tea slowly sipped in rented rooms with rows of bookshelves on sunny afternoons by the sea, where rats roam freely like bookworms—"*un rat de bibli*"—they too reasonless and quite pointless until lab day. But even the reasonless rose grows, alas, for another one's nose.

THE SEERS
BY THE SEA

The seers stand lined up by the sea, with long, black dresses fluttering in the wind and fingering the sand. Their sockets are hollow, for the seers do not see. Their hair descends to their waists, and their knotty hands with pointy fingers extend toward the customer who has just shown up on the shore. First, they make him undress. Then, they dress him in salt and algae. With hungry hands they open his skull, unbraiding the brain, smoothing its creases and unrolling the twisted dwellings of memory. They unroll and unroll, undoing the work of time, going up the river of hours and erasing all traces. For, in order to see the future, one pays by losing the past.

TURTLE TEARS

"Stop giving water to the mice!" they used to tell us in the abandoned language. Or else: "crying with turtle tears." Or was it "crocodile tears"? Crocodile tears streamed down our cheeks as we ate our peppery-hot, steamy turtle soup. They also told us: "No use crying for yesterday." Yet we cried, again and again, for yesterday and over spilled turtle soup, we ate and we cried, we cried and we ate our peppery-hot, steamy turtle soup, and collected our crocodile tears in elegant alligator purses, while mice bathed in the bathwater of our tears. By the time we finished eating, we had ourselves become little turtles wrapped in perfectly round shells. We were tortoise shells collecting tears on rainy days, when the clouds cried for yesterday and for tomorrow, though it was no use. No use crying over spilled rain, but the clouds cried again and again with crocodile tears streaming down houses and trees, and saved for dark days in our abandoned turtle shells. And we kept eating our peppery-hot, steamy turtle soup in the light days born of our unending turtle tears.

RED HOODS AND SUGAR DOLLS

At the hospital for sugar dolls little girls are allowed to stay overnight, providing they refrain from eating them. They are given gingerbread hearts to chew on, while gingerly attending to the dolls, and their pink heart-shaped mouths let out echoes that intoxicate the dry, white walls. The echoes are of nothing—not of words, but of other echoes, like mirrors endlessly reflecting images of other images. As they hold their precious sugar dolls, the girls seem as sweet as the objects of their affection, yet the empty echoes spilling out of them are ropes circling the nurses' necks and pulled by unseen hands. The girls wear little red hoods, though this may be an optical illusion of the guardian's eye in charge of watching over them at night. At night, the eye sees how the red hoods melt into pure *red*, the color red floating in the air with no shape to hang on to, no *I* to take refuge in. This pure red of I-less beings soon dissolves into faint echoes of pale colors until it settles into unmistakable white.

Old Poets Waiting on Death Row

for F. A. Nettelbeck

"Old poets waiting on death throwing snowballs at the sun." Old poets waiting on death throwing up at the sun. Old sons wailing at death rowing up in the snow. Old swans wooing death soaring up and down. Odd balls pawning death roaring at old nuns. Bald poets towing death snoring loud. No poets throwing pots and pans at death in the snow. Old poets weeping throwing darts at snow walls. No death pawing when rolling down the lawn! No pawns waiting on death blabbing sunsense now! No balls thrown down at old poets by nonsense nuns! No sense knowing death warped by trapeze laws! Old traps waiting on poets dwarfing dawns. Dawns dawning on death waiting on and on. Death waiting on death. Waiting on.

THE SPIDER'S GOD

A spider weaves a web whose center, a black point from where white rays interlace in maze-like configurations, is himself. His web is at once his work, his play, his art, his home. If he had a religion, his web would also be his God. He would probably think that he has been condemned to eternal labor and that to end means to kill God. His home would be a temple enclosing God's spirit as in a tomb. He would live with the anguishing knowledge that his life's goal is God's death, that creating means killing, and that there is no other way. But very likely, the spider has no religion and no God. Work-play-art-home, he is simply an integrated being.

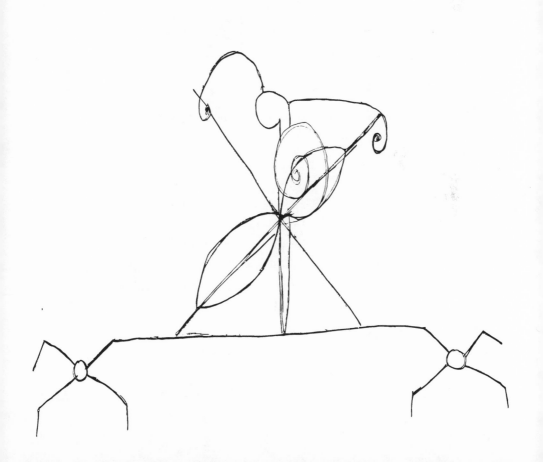

À LA
GEORGES PEREC

"You'd think it's a sound coming from a rotting corps'
cursing us."

—*A Void*

So G. P. says. And adds that it sounds as if coming from
downstairs, though it could spring from who knows what
part. It jumps, mounts and climbs stairs, and rolls across halls,
similar to snowballs. But it's a ball of sounds, a soundball full with
loud words. G. P. also says that pinning sounds on walls has strongly
hurt not his musings but his musical spirit. And thus quit playing
with words and sounds, only to find painting. But as G. P. took a
brush and sat by his canvas, his brush did again what his ballpoint
tip always did: it built words. Tombs for living words. But now in

colors with a virtual soundtrack. Mounting from a void in which black ribbons float without accompanying signs, words mirror colors, and crying colors twirl, swirl and spin down dry hills, as if tumbling ad infinitum within dark clocks that show sounds not hours. Coats hang on worn-out hands at four cardinal points, and a child laughs showing a putrid throat. Moths occasionally visit said coats, as idiots in the city plaza gasp, rolling big I-balls, which fall on floors, and black shadows walk up and down, crushing on and on. Through a door ajar, a young lady shows, chopping onion, garlic, stirring pots, putting in a pinch of salt, moving about, with blond hair down to waist. A cook or this building's boss? A lady or a lad in drag? Laughing child—from abov'—puts his hand on lady's butt, but lady hits him with a wood'n spoon. It is noon. Much too soon to say if night's sky will show stars or just a black void. For now, G. P. puts his brush down: all is blank.

THE STORY OF THE A-LESS PORCUPINE

I know of one little fellow, whose round body looks like zero. When he is cornered, he coils unto himself, yet he's no turtle; he shows thorns, yet he's no rose; he twirls & tumbles, yet he's no bush or shrub, but he's got hedge in his hog; his body mirrors open flowers, yet he's everclosed. If he could choose some concubine, she would rhyme with him. He lives in the woods of Montsouris, yet he's got no mouse, though he somehow looks like one. He pines for something he's been missing, yet he ignores the *a*-lessness of his illness. He longs to fill his void with my story, yet the story [*a*]voids him. It empties him of his needles, of his endless *a*-lessness. He is forever *a*-less, ever more less, lessfull. Whether French or English, he is *a*-less: hérisson-hedgehog, porc-épic-porcupine.

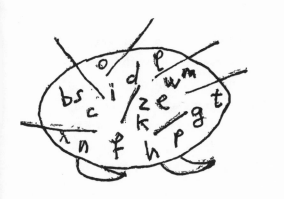

TRILINGUAL POEM WITH DEAD SWANS

Lebede moarte pe ape vinete—*Cygnes morts dans des eaux violettes*—**Dead swans on purple waters**—tremura albe de iarna—*tremblent blancs d'hiver*—**shiver white with winter**—sufletele li s-au exilat pe luna—*leurs âmes se sont enfuies dans la lune*—**their souls have run away on the moon**—ochii li s-au topit in ceata de smoala—*leurs yeux ont fondu dans la brume de suie*—**their eyes have melted in the fog of soot**—lebede moarte transformate în carte—*cygnes morts mués en signes*—**dead swans now signs.**

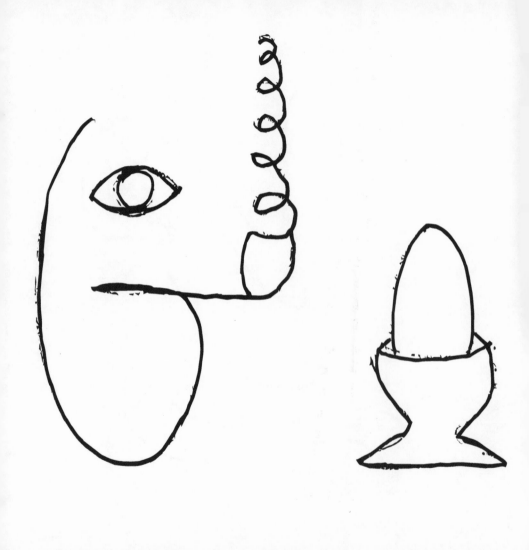

AN
EGGCENTRIC MAN

He is an eggcentric man. I'd ask him, "What's cooking?" and he'd answer, "Don't play balls with me." I'd ask, "How do you like your eggs?" and he'd say, "Hard up" or "Side over" or "Siam-easy." I'd ask, "Fried, boiled or scrambled?" and he'd say, "Foibled" or "Broiled" or "Scrabbled." I'd ask, "Would you care for an eggcup?" and he'd say, "Egghead is your mother's daughter, egghead." I'd ask, "Salt or pepper?" and he'd say, "You're such a pest, sister." I'd ask, "How about an omelet?" and he'd say, "Let me beat your eyewhites first." I'd ask, "Have you lost your season?" and he'd say, "Save your eggcracks for your wisetimer. Crack your time with wisecracker. Time your cracks with wise off." I'd ask, "Are you nut?" and he'd say, "A nutcracker for a woodpecker. Crack your wood and peck your nut." Finally, eggsasperated, I'd ask, "Do you like polenta with eggs?" and he'd say, "Your legs drive me woods. If you egg on my pen into your nut, I'll let you plant your egg in my woods." And then I'd say nothing, for he is truly a most centric eggman.

Water and Time

Water running inside time splashing and gurgling away from its source salt floating inside water shining through sheer transparency tears dried inside salt away from face of clay earth dried inside clay staining potter's hands round vase out of clay filling his cupped hands water inside vase filling clay-face-salt-water-time. Time running inside water running inside time.

TIME INSIDE OUT

I am running out of time, he said, then fell inside it. He struggled to get out, but soon it was twelve o' clock, and a chatty cuckoo came out to tell the hour. He thought that if he could set the clock's hands at zero, he could get out, but soon it was midnight and he fell back in all over again. He ran inside time in ever bigger circles, as the cuckoo told the time, and each time he thought he was out, midnight struck, and again he ran out of time.

SONG OF THE ROOSTER

He runs with shoes of lavender lace in the fields of ghost potatoes. He unzips the corners of his mouth three times before daybreak and words spill out drenched in red anguish. He is a minstrel of morning trapped in a bureaucrat's body. His song at the edge of night and silence dreams of a shape pulled toward light.

And so on Sundays we use the salt of our tears for rooster stew, dipping into the salt of memory, and roosterless but saltful the liquid night spills into the light of day that never breaks.

THE ECHO GIRL

The Echo Girl is always second. She lags behind, a trail of sounds on her footsteps. Her voice is a necklace of grains of sand at no one's neck. When the teacher asks a question, she looks him in the eye and repeats it. The teacher is annoyed. "What a pain," he whispers, and the girl, after him: "What a pain, what a pain." The teacher grows increasingly infuriated. He concentrates, comes up with a different question, and the girl repeats it after him. "What an idiot," he says, and the girl, after him: "What an idiot, what an idiot." Now, the teacher is so furious he would like to strangle the girl. His fingers extend like a hungry octopus toward the girl's neck, but she is quicker than he, and before he touches her, she bursts into air, followed by a trail of empty laughter.

THE HOUSE OF LAUGHTER

The House of Laughter is guarded by a dwarf the left side of whose face cries, and whose right side laughs. In the House of Laughter there are no comedians with stale jokes written by monocellular Sybarites. Whoever enters the house first needs to learn the joy of tears, and pluck them raw from the trees circling the house. Every Sunday the tear trees put out a red fruit in the shape of a heart—no one's heart. Under the tree of no one's heart the dwarf plays the harmonica, so round with contentment, so pink with bliss that when he laughs the house's walls collapse, and laughter spills into the world, and you and I and he and she can laugh. When laughter is, the house is not.

WHAT WE DID WITH SHLOMO

N o one in the family loved Shlomo. I realize that this statement alone may be enough to trigger your sympathy, but you have no reason to be sympathetic. When I met Shlomo, he was an eighty-year-old lecherous man with a syrupy gaze in which every woman who happened to pass by got stuck like a fly on a sticky surface. We couldn't keep a kitchen helper or a nurse for more than a month. He pursued them all with an indiscriminate taste that made me sometimes wonder whether I should feel offended because I was the only woman he never made a pass at. The nurses were for his companion, to whom I was closely related—though the exact nature of our family ties shall remain undisclosed.

You have probably understood by now that Shlomo was not related to us by blood. He came into the family shortly after the death of the aforementioned relative's husband. For fifteen years we saw him at family gatherings, Thanksgivings, bar mitzvahs, birthdays, anniversaries and, of course, whenever we visited his companion. Eventually we got used to him. What could we do? We even forgave him for being a Republican—the only one in the family.

But when he died—barely a year after the death of his companion—we were suddenly faced with a dilemma: what will we do with Shlomo? As long as he was alive, he could take good care of himself, even if that meant living on Scotch and cigarettes. He was a jolly fellow, and when his time came, he looked at death without bitterness or regret. So did we.

But the question was: what were we to do with his remains? We were left with a small, heavy box full of ashes, and none of us was eager to take possession of it, or at least, to take it somewhere—a hill, a beach—and spread its contents there. We all shivered in disgust when we were asked; disgust at the mere thought of accidentally spilling the ashes on ourselves.

Thus the box remained in a dark nook of the hidden bar where Shlomo kept his Scotch. The house was put on the market and eventually sold to a family of newly arrived Palestinian immigrants. At our next family reunion everyone joked: "That should serve him right! Eternal life with the Palestinians!"

You see, like most of the family, Shlomo was Jewish. But the joke is, of course, double-sided, for the Palestinians who bought the house and proceeded immediately to its restoration will never know that, as in old creation myths about bridges and cathedrals built on a human life walled up in them, their house was founded on a Jew buried in a bar.

A WORKSHOP IN SAUSAGES

The girls sat at the big, rectangular table with the teacher, also female, at one end. The day's theme: "sausages." In the middle of the table, a huge, brown, moist, slightly upward curved sausage presided under the frightened eyes of the nubile audience. The sausage's owner, a blondish girl of delicate frame sat at the other end of the table. "What is it about this sausage that you find compelling?" asked the teacher, and the girls answered with prolonged silence. Nothing in their sheltered lives had prepared them for an encounter with such a big, brown, moist, slightly upward curved sausage. As they sat watching in silence, something stirred inside the star-sausage and it began to move, barely perceptibly at first, then more and more visibly, in a way that could only be described as "insolent." "It doesn't behave in a way that one would expect from a sausage," one of the girls said, and the teacher approved. The other girls looked at her, jealous that they didn't think of that. Then something unexplainable happened: another sausage fell from somewhere, and soon it began to rain sausages, big and small, moist or dry, and the girls took refuge under the table. The teacher tried to keep a cool composure, assuring them that all was fine, yet her trembling voice betrayed her nervousness in regard to a situation none of her manuals mentioned or taught her how to handle. One doesn't expect a sausage to behave in such a way. Without haste, as if to prove that nothing was out of order, the teacher joined the girls under the table and tried to continue the conversation, which wasn't easy because there were sausages everywhere, in their mouths even, and how is one to have an intelligent discussion with a sausage in one's mouth?

And so the girls choked on sausages, as the sausage on the table, the Original one, swelled and swelled until it filled the entire room, which is now open only for a special session of the graduate seminar on "How to write about a sausage without objectifying it."

THE CHILDREN'S THEATER

In the Town-Where-Nothing-Ever-Happens schoolteachers take the children on weekends to the Children's Theater for plays, movies, musicals and other shows. During holidays, the Children's Theater shows movies made for children only, and dozens of children from all over the town are crammed into the suffocating hall, waiting for the doors to open, the older and stronger ones—mostly boys—pushing their way ahead through the crowd with their elbows and kicks to the joints of the younger kids. When the doors open, the mass of children in the hall—a huge mollusk made of dozens of bodies glued together—moves forward with a new surge of energy, breaking through the glass doors and leaving behind pieces of chewed caramel, handkerchiefs, multicolored wrapping foil, spit and blood. Then the theater staff collects the dead bodies of the little children crushed by the older and stronger ones.

Finally, the survivors are in, on the cozy chairs of blue plush—though some chairs are plastic and others, vandalized, show their innards made of some creamy, foamy matter. The lights are out and the show kicks off. A man appears on the stage and begins to sing a hit pop song, while colored lights twinkle here and there, and white steam is released for special effects. The children grow increasingly excited. The steam, particularly, seems to please them. They eat popcorn, sunflower and pumpkin seeds, whose shells they spit on the floor. One kid throws a candy at the singer, but misses him. Inspired, another one throws his notebook on stage, still missing the singer, who appears more and more nervous. Soon, all the children are throwing things—candies, crumpled paper, paper airplanes, eggs, pebbles. A more creative boy unzips his pants and directs a perfect semicircle of yellow pee toward the same target, but can only reach the kids several rows down, who in turn, unzip their pants, thus creating a domino effect that plunges a whole area of the theater into wet chaos. On stage, the singer is covered in a gooey film, a paper plane on his head, but keeps singing. The children's excitement has reached paroxysm—they tap their feet, yelling and laughing hysterically. When the show is over, the staff comes to pick up the singer's body from under the heap amassed on stage, while the children trickle out, humming the tune they have just learned, happy, innocent.

TRUTH

She is four-and-a-half years old, five at most. She lives in a country whose gray walls have more ears than all its citizens together. Her kindergarden is adjacent to a prison whose inmates, dressed in gray clothes, can be spotted by the children as they take their breaks in the courtyard.

One day, a teacher with a gray face, dressed in a gray suit, told the children that they would soon be visited by the county's Department of Education inspectors, and that it was very important for them to give the right answers. So the teacher taught the children both the questions and the answers, which they repeated many times until they knew them by heart. Question: "Who is the man who builds our bridges, schools and hospitals?" Answer: "Comrade C., President of our Socialist Republic, General Secretary of the Communist Party." Question: "Who is the dearest Parent of all our country's children?" Answer: "Comrade C., President of our Socialist Republic, General Secretary of the Communist Party." And so on.

There were several questions, but there was only one answer, so it wasn't very difficult for the children to memorize it.

When the inspectors come, their suits aren't gray, they are black. Maybe it's their suits, maybe their huge bellies—something in their appearance must have frightened the children, for, when summoned by the teacher, they all stare blankly, in dumb silence. The inspectors leave, and the teacher begins to scream at the children, furious that none of them had been able to give the correct answer. The little girl raises her hand. "I knew the answer, I just didn't want to say it," she declares. The teacher is puzzled. "Why?" "Because it isn't the truth."

Law No. 29

E veryone knew Law No. 29. Or rather, everyone was familiar with Law No. 29, for in truth, no one *knew* it. You see, Law No. 29 was a stroke of genius of the most enlightened member of the country's Communist Party, its General Secretary, also known as the "Genius of the Carpathians," the "Dear Leader" or, more modestly, the "Dear Parent." Law No. 29, also called the "Secret Law," had no…content. Or rather, its content was secret for reasons of "state security," as they told us. Yet people could, and were in fact arrested and found guilty of having transgressed a law whose content no one knew. Anyone at any moment could be found guilty of breaking the invisible law.

When in December 1989 the regime fell, shattering to pieces with such boisterous clamor on the glass floors of the invisible cells of the ever-present rulers, and the people took over the secret police's headquarters, the first thing they did was to find out what the famous law said. Wanting to know the reason for which they had been punished all those years, they opened one of the enormous files labeled "State Secret," the kind of files that can only be found in labyrinthine stomachs of invisible whales, and read:

"Law No. 29. The Communist Party and its General Secretary are hereby declaring this to be Law No. 29: *'Anyone found guilty of breaking Law No. 29 will be punished according to Law No. 29.'*"

In their anger, the people stepped on the heavy files, crumpling the pages and tearing them apart, once again breaking the law whose open secret was known to anyone who had ever broken it.

THE CHIMNEY SWEEPER

Even after he disappeared, swallowed by the mythology of the past, his name and image remained in songs and in those pins with white and red thread we used to put on our chest to welcome spring. Those tiny brooches in metal or plastic called *martzisoare*—that is, "little marches," named for March—represented flowers, little hearts, birds, usually a symbol of something, in the same way the little marches themselves stood for spring. A symbol of a symbol. The white thread stood for winter and the red one for summer. The fruit of their fight was spring. The chimney sweeper was one of the most popular little marches, for it too stood for something: luck. Its blackness was turned into its opposite, white—luck. Excrements were also a sign of luck. On the other hand, running into a priest was like running into the devil or a black cat. One had to cross oneself, spit and take three steps back. One also had to spit three times on a baby whose cuteness triggered admiration, in order to chase away the evil eye.

Funny, this was supposed to be a poem about a chimney sweeper and it became a story about what one can find if one looks down the chimney. Like those children in a Dickens novel, used by evil, greedy men to sweep chimneys, who fall down the dark, narrow tunnel only to come back years later in white suits, rich, happy, accompanied by the sister they lost at birth.

Ashes and Cinnamon

The Sunday strolls on the Corso—the main downtown street where the traffic stopped on weekends—smelled of vanilla and tasted like ice cream. The city's "working class"—as they said on TV and in the papers—was out in its Sunday best, the men in their suits, the women in their colorful dresses. Vendors on the sidewalk sold ice-cream cones and cotton candy, which we called "sugar-on-a-stick," and the little girl watched in fascination as the latter unfolded its ghostly body of gauze. Her favorite ice cream was "chocolate ice-cream-on-a-stick," a kind she's never seen since, with the mass of ice cream like a reed's brown, elongated top. Ice cream was a Sunday ritual, as she was usually not to have any: a fragile child prone to frequent colds.

And then there were the vendors that appeared years later with their hot dogs, which everyone called "dicks-in-a-bun" because the bun was scooped out and the hot dog was stuck inside upwards like a virile member with mustard all around. But that was later, and by then the ice-cream-on-a-stick and the sugar-on-a-stick had disappeared, as did the smell of vanilla and the Sunday suits. And now the Corso is made of layers of disintegrated bubbles of time, a layer of cinnamon and one of ashes, with the ashes gradually covering everything, and the cinnamon retreating in memory's cellars for future excavations.

WEDDING IN THE
BALKANS

There, weddings are made of different time-stuff. They begin with a contest: first, the two mothers-in-law spit out all the curses they've accumulated in a lifetime, from "May you burn in Hell with all your family and the children of your children," to "May your mouth go dry and your tongue go rotten," the latter, the worst of all, for how is one to curse with a dry mouth and a rotten tongue? For hours they spit out their venom, exorcising all the demons, until the two families are purified and their children can unite.

But this time, the bride's mother said something different, something no one expected. "May you never forget," she said, and then the other woman stopped, with the curse stuck on her lips, unable to let it go.

Later in the day, the procession left the bride's house, she in her long, white gown, and the female guests in their colorful dresses, with the paid jester telling one obscene joke after another, thus working up the crowd before they would arrive at the groom's house where the couple was to be locked up in the bridal chamber while the crowd waited by the door and eventually exploded in cheers, as the groom emerged holding up like a flag the white bloodstained sheet.

But this time, the procession left with the bride while the groom waited with his own folk, and waited and waited, and the bride never arrived. Snowflakes big as daisies had begun to fall on the bride's procession—though it was summer—and an icy wind started to blow, carrying away the women's straw hats, pulling up their skirts and unveiling their legs, and they walked like this for hours without getting anywhere, and then for days, and their hair grew white with icicles and their feet stumbled in the snow that was now up to their knees, and they walked for weeks and for months, until they could move no longer.

And the groom waited a whole year until someone brought the news that a group of cheerful wedding guests had been spotted in the mountains, time-frozen into statues of snow, and one could still see the crystal glasses in their hands with the frozen red wine, and the frozen smiles on their faces, and the bride's gown barely distinguishable on the white background. And the groom ordered a painting to be made after the frozen *tableau mort* from what had once been *nature vivante*, and he never forgot.

Why They Call It the Old World

I t is not for nothing that they call it the Old World. In her grandparents' village things are the way they were hundreds of years ago. Some Western journalists say that many people regret communism, but they understand nothing. What people regret is not communism, but the past. In that part of the world the past is always better. For scarves, they wrap around their necks streams of blood passed on from generation to generation, and they lament the old days. So much so that when the villagers in her grandparents' village had to elect their mayor, the majority re-elected the old mayor in spite of an insurmountable handicap: the man was no longer of this world. In an interview, a villager explained, "I know he's dead, but I don't want any change."

American Girls on Campus

They edge past her with muscled legs and solar hair, their eyes turned inward toward nothing, though they think of nothingness as a creepy old woman they will never be. They sparkle. They look at each other as in a mirror beyond which nothing else exists. In daytime they read books that tell them how to live a happy life without a man; at night they dream of the day when, dressed in white lace dotted with pink hearts, they proceed toward flowery altars where a hairy Italian man greets them with French kisses. When they talk with boys they giggle and push forward their low-cut décolletages stuffed with borrowed flesh, and their gestures emanate the liquid femininity of corn syrup—though they hate the word "femininity." At parties their high-pitched voices merge into a silver film of soporific vapors, out of which emerge colored ribbons, high energy chocolate bars, self-improvement manuals, how-to guides dismissing self-improvement manuals, how-to guides dismissing how-to guides. At school they read the French feminists, at home *The Cosmopolitan.* They are the daughters of a couple framed in a picture whose painter is a man born to a Puritan woman wrapped in a shawl of stale prayers, and to a bearded man called Freud, who enjoyed looking under her skirt. The painter has committed suicide, and the painted couple kept within itself the split of its creator, which the daughters have also inherited. They keep their skirts tight so no bearded man can peep underneath, but underneath there is no secret. They are the guardians of the-place-with-no-secret.

Dancing with D.

She was a woman of a certain age, dark skinned, her hair drawn back and graying at the temples, with hollowed cheeks and violet circles under the deep set eyes, and a mouth of withered sensuality, slightly parted, as her body undulated slowly in the echoing rhythm of the melody coming from some remote location. She was long past her youth, but far from trying to hide it. When she moved she put forward her age with the seductive shamelessness of a young Gypsy. Her discreet but enveloping obscenity was what attracted him to her, so he took her in his arms and they began a slow dance, their gazes locked, and as she moved, she grew lighter and lighter, her body a mere skeleton with its bones rattling in step with the music, and suddenly he understood that he was dancing with Death. But by then it was too late.

Bilingual Poem
avec Clichés

"*Danse avec moi* under the stormy sky"
— Daniel Lanois

*D*anse avec moi baby under the stormy sky move your hips like a pro we have left our *motos chez les pompiers rue de l'Apocalypse* and now we have to go *chez le dentiste* to take my heart out *danse avec moi* stay with me *chez les pompiers* to put out my fire *ne me quitte pas* dance with me *sous la pluie* today I found a letter from my landlord *et me voilà maintenant dans la rue* and the rain keeps falling on my *violon sur mon trombone mon saxophone* oh baby *suis-je donc la mariée* who left her groom in Silverspoon *suis-je donc la mariée qui pleure* under the stormy sky *tels les sanglots longs des violons* stay with me *pour la vie* oh baby

USED WORDS

A room full of furniture. Start by taking every single piece out, and when nothing is left but the bare walls, stare at them until all you can see is white, and a taste of plaster and brick settles on your tongue. Swallow, and fill your bones with the walls' white emptiness. Swallow, and imagine that now you take out every single one of your bones, whose bluish whiteness echoes the bare walls. Close your eyes and imagine that your brain is a piggy-bank turned upside-down, out of which words are dropping like coins. When all the coins will have been dropped and you are filled with emptiness, when you are empty of bones and empty of words, maybe you can begin writing. Until then, just stare at the wall. As honestly as you can.

ON WRITING

Writing is always a betrayal. Of what one writes about and wants to say but cannot; and of what one brings to light but should have remained unspoken. Never trust writers who write about what is essential to them: they wouldn't refrain from using anything and anyone in order to serve the higher order of Words. On the other hand, writers who write about anything else aren't real writers.

BEAUTY

What can Beauty ask from life? It always asks for warm blood—or rather, the one watching Beauty always asks for blood, when in fact, Beauty is cold and makes a mockery of life. The very fact that one likes to *watch* Beauty is a sign of Beauty's lifelessness. Of course, Beauty's incarnations we like to watch are always alive, but we love them not for their aliveness; we love them for their very detachment from life. We love them because they are so *separate* from us, so *other*, and yet, in the mirror of our eyes, so much like us, that is, if "us" were a picture of us. We love Beauty in others because no matter how much we extend our hand it always comes back empty. We love Beauty because deep down all we want is to own nothing, for, if there is something that cannot be owned, it is Beauty. We love Beauty because we want nothing, nothing at all.

LOVE

It is something that exists only in books. We build bridges to the realm of No One, knowing fully well that no one is there. Yet we build them again and again, with our eyes fixed on no one, hoping for our love to be returned by no one. Even if no one were someone, we would still be loved by no one. That's why I always preferred (exceptions notwithstanding) to love the dead and people who don't exist. That's why, in other words, I am always in love with my own head.

(Un)Happiness

Could it be that you are always so unhappy because you despise happiness? Even if that were so, it would not explain why you are so unhappy—after all, you don't despise happiness that much. Could it be that you are so unhappy because you believe that happiness is a lie—but in that case, unhappiness is also a lie. Or maybe it is because you have too much time to think about your degree of happiness, in which case you certainly are happier than most people. But if that were so, most people will have already died of unhappiness, and not only do they continue to thrive, but when you look around every single one of them seems happier than you. Do they pretend to be happy? It is doubtful. Who would they attempt to convince? Maybe, on the contrary, *you* are the one always pretending to be unhappy (you know, all those nineteenth century novels you've read) when, in fact, you are quite happy. Then why do you feel so unhappy? Why do you keep moving in circles like a trapped fly waiting for the spider? Why do you want to be both the spider and the fly, and keep weaving this net of empty words in a room full of mirrors? Maybe this is what unhappiness is: to live in a room full of mirrors and to be incapable, absolutely incapable of breaking them.

BLACKNESS STRANGENESS

Blackness. Holes of blackness filling time with strangeness. Strange estranged strangled with a thread of hope beyond hopelessness. Parting with everything. Departing stranger filled with blackness neither now nor tomorrow nor ever. Black fever surrounding everything so strange so far away. Sorrow. So utterly black in this blinding light filled with strangeness. So strange to feel so light and yet be full of darkness. Such a stranger to one's own self self self severed from everything. Hanging on a thread of hope from a cloud filled with blackness.

ALTA IFLAND is the author of a bilingual (French-English) book of prose poems, *Voix de Glace/Voice of Ice* (Les Figues Press), which was awarded the French prize Louis Guillaume, and two collections of short stories, *Elegy for a Fabulous World* (Ninebark Press, finalist of the Northern California Book Award) and *Death-in-a-Box* (Subito Press, winner of the Subito Fiction Prize). She lives in California.

S P U Y T E N   D U Y V I L
Meeting Eyes Bindery
Triton